Ivy Alvarez

DISTURBANCE

SEREN

Seren is the book imprint of
Poetry Wales Press Ltd.
57 Nolton Street, Bridgend, Wales, CF31 3AE
www.serenbooks.com
Facebook: facebook.com/SerenBooks
Twitter: @SerenBooks

The right of Ivy Alvarez to be identified as
the author of this work has been asserted in accordance
with the Copyright, Designs and Patents Act, 1988.

ISBN: 978-1-78172-087-5
e-book ISBN: 978-1-78172-089-9
Kindle ISBN: 978-1-78172-088-2

A CIP record for this title is available from the British Library.

The publisher acknowledges the financial assistance of the Welsh Books Council.

*This book is an imaginative retelling of and a response to actual events.
It does not purport to be a documentary work, a factual account or a work of record.
Names, actions and thoughts of the characters are products of the author's imagination
and are used fictitiously.*

Cover image: Matthew Albanese, 'Burning Room'
Wood, nylon, plexiglass, purchased dollhouse furniture
www.matthewalbanese.com

Printed in Bembo by CPI Group (UK) Limited, Croydon

Author's Website: www.ivyalvarez.com

Contents

Inquest

Members of the family wept
as the coroner read out
her pleas for help.

Nothing softened as they cried.
The wood in the room stayed hard
and square.

The windows clear.
The stenographer impassive.
The spider under the bench
intent on its fly.

Nuclear family

One mansion
worth one million
or nine hundred
seventy-five thousand
depending on the newspaper

For sale at nine hundred
and eighty-five thousand

An ex-employee files a lawsuit
for three hundred
and sixty-one thousand

One life
insurance policy worth three
hundred thousand

Thirty-six thousand cash
in the BMW, plus one
bottle of JD, a number of cable ties,
plastic bottles filled with petrol,
one pair of scissors

They met 27 years ago

One injunction
One divorce

One emergency number
dialled at 7.11 pm

Fourteen cartridges
from a twelve-gauge shotgun
reloaded seven times

Five neighbours
beg to differ

One son
shot five times
in the chest and back

One mother
shot four times
in the chest and lower back

One man
with a gunshot wound
to the head

A coroner, police constable,
superintendent, detective inspector
and domestic violence co-ordinator
circle the scene

One daughter
left alive
releases her statement

Operator

My dinner rests warm in my belly.
I've just come in for my shift.
Familiar smell of old coffee,
stale sweat accumulates,
hovers near the ceiling.
My chair warms to my presence.
Already I can't wait to leave.
The lights blink, the phone rings.
I'm here 'til two in the morning.
Breakfast before dawn. Then sleep.

The phone rings: laughter and shrieks.
Another crank call, two cranks in ten minutes.
I just got here.

The minute hand swings over.
It's 7.11 pm.

'What is the nature
of your emergency?'
Weariness
wears my voice.

But then she speaks.
I type quickly. I press buttons.

'What is your address?'
The pads of my fingers prickle,
become slick. Keys slip beneath my skin.

Her breath
catches.   Thunder blooms
behind her voice
– once, twice. Her scream
pierces my ear.

'I have got officers on the way.'
My voice is steady. My hands shake.
She whispers to me. I barely understand.

'Where is he now?'
I punch buttons. The minute hand
wipes the clock's face.

'We have got people coming up.'
She whimpers and cries.
Her fear is salty. I taste
its metal. I taste her tears.

'Just stay where you are
– keep hidden.'
I feel the tremor of my jaw.

Two more gunshots.
I don't scream, though I want to.
I keep talking.

'Are you upstairs?'
She cries.
She cries.

I hear a door opening.
I hear her cry out.

The line goes dead.

The Journalist speaks I

There are details I can report.
Others I can only guess at.

as always
I arrive too late for witnessing
must rein myself in
must not mention
how the neighbour was ignored
the evidence overlooked

the time that elapsed
between when she hit the button for help
and when the police arrived

omit the pictures of her body in the cupboard
how her husband tracked her blood around like the sun
                    red radiant

before he came to rest
his brains
              a blood halo

how their son had died
his arm by his side
the frost on his skin disappearing

his frozen look of surprise

while the police did not
              would not say *sorry*
they wore the apology in their eyes
as they took their bodies far from the crime site

The good neighbour

That For Sale sign was put up a while ago. They were quiet neighbours and very nice. We thought something was wrong – we didn't know they were breaking up their home. I couldn't say. You wouldn't've looked twice at them. She was quiet. What do I know? We keep to ourselves. Lived here long? No. They moved in two years ago. Paid a cheap price for the house. It's worth a million now – so I've been told. That right? Yes, I think so. You've been inside? Did you see their bodies? Oh, don't tell me. Why I asked, I don't know. It was a mistake that slipped out just now. Please, can we leave it there? I'd like you to go. Just don't write I asked about their bodies. My husband can answer that. I don't know.

The estate agents

she came to us
don't forget
court-appointed
out of our hands

we are not ghouls
we are estate agents

the house was valued
at less than one million
we tried to sell it
at nine eighty-five

fifteen thousand shy
of a million

off the record?
five thousand per dead body
but we don't look at it
that way

the damage to the house
was cosmetic and extensive

it took ages to prise
the buckshot from the walls
the blood from the floors
such stubborn stains

no, no-one's bought it
but it's early days yet

A neighbouring farmer

how to prepare
for the slaughter of lambs
   the stunning of cows
the blood as it pools on the floor
disappears down a hole

   the news of three people
who've died
divested of their animal hides
      their animate lives

   the white flesh of pigs
the bristle
the gristle
the bones

the chambered heart

something written in the blood

I've watched a body
make certain
accommodations
for intrusions
of bolt bullet knife

this is what I've learnt

I don't know what could have set him off

then again
I cannot understand
how cows know
to chew in unison

they watch me when I feed them
eyes like his

what else can flip out
like he did

a hinged lid

anybody

anything can set me off
the smell of earth and shit
the boots' rubber edge
as it rubs away
the back of my calves
the back of my hand
across my lids
sometimes I get mad
especially at sheep
they're so stupid
loving me
even as I kill them

and who could love a cow
with the teeter-totter of calves
        madness and brain fever
the Swiss cheese holes
eating coordination
they splay on spindle legs
and fall
without grace

I am split
open-skinned
red
with death

scratch the chickens between their legs
there's the egg
glowing like a secret

I didn't really know him
only to wave to

he'd buy from me
his dozen eggs
commiserate
about my cows
when madness took to them
like an amorous bull

anyone could go that way
he said
I think he did

he leaned on the fence
and gazed
at the many fires
    the indelible smoke's
black brush stroke
dipping into night
reading its script
something I could not see

The neighbour at no. 51

she sent a Christmas card last year –
marital problems in fine copperplate

how would I know?
I live alone

their house, always full of shouts
slammed doors and screams

I don't like to be seen
as a nosy neighbour

I closed the curtains
turned off the lights

nudged the shade
aside

my eyes grew used
to dark and light

I heard him then
he wanted to get in

he ranted and roared –
the last I saw of him

was in his car
brooding in the dark

afterwards
I heard the shots

but I didn't think it came from him
from somewhere else maybe

I don't know how many
really

it's none of my concern, I thought –
and I try not to think about it

The neighbour's daughter

Father shielded me from the shouts, the rifle's
dark sound. The trees whispered
complicity, complicity. I ran

inside. I looked outside at Tom. *That's Tom,*
I said. Father called for help. His words, cold
stones dropping down a well. Water dripped time

down a hole. The bathroom tiles stared back: blank
and clinical as blood into soil feeds
the trees, who look on... their lungs sigh, their leaves.

Husband, interrupted

spoon of my self
I am convex
and concave

the tarnish and rub
of supper
gunshots in the dark

my wife knifes the ribs
meticulous
as a doe

venison on plates
gravy in a boat
my nerves sing of tines and forks

I lick my lips of supper sauce

I am stained
cars wait to be chased
like dogs

peas in my concavity
butter slippery
calm and digestible

the thin pitch of cutlery
high sirens
outside my door

overhead
my security light
as if I had a clue

the night is full of singing stars
oboe shadows
out of tune

my wife cries
at supper's ruin
there's too much shouting
when the cops come marching in

Paternal Grandfather

my skin, my bones, my eyes, my lips
this tongue, my words, my tears, my spit
I say nothing is definite

this gravity, this soil, those trees,
this wind, my son's gun, his wife's blood
their son's blood, their shouts echo, fade

my blood, my veins, your tongue, your words
these questions, all of it – nothing

Maternal Grandfather

no I don't sleep
old age wants me awake
conscious but weary
vigorous and tough
or pretending well enough
too much bad news comes
you have to be vigilant
or you'll shatter
we are all shattered
a phone rings in the middle
of your life
three lives gone in one night
when I drop my cup
I am shattered by it
I was not watchful enough
though I stayed awake all night
waiting

Grandmother: interview

Worn surfaces reveal too much –
an open wound, a patch of earth,
the cavity in one's mouth – don't
you find? Get a rug; hides bloodstains,
my neighbour said. Yes, I loved him,
my son, but liked? No. As a child,
he'd cling to my thighs, dig right in.
Oh, his love just wore me right out.

How was I to know he would take
a life or two? His wife, his son?
How could I know? What could I do?
We thought they were happy. Their house
was so new. Everything paid for.
Nothing owed. Oh, what do I know?
It's obvious I don't. I feel
just horrible. Like it's my fault.

He was desperate to go home
but there's nothing for it, is there?
If one's home does not want you back?
He loved her so. Maybe too much....
Did he hurt her? I don't know. Oh,
what about the stains? Who's going
to clean that up? I'll buy a rug.
It's the least we can do. The least.

The Journalist speaks II

I'm here to throw rocks
mar the glass
jar the faces

I ask my questions
extract details
take these flesh gobbets
to feed the hounds

condense doubt from the air
gather witnesses and catch their breath
perform my ordinary alchemy
subtracting emotion
distilling facts

look at the splash of blood
make it black and white
coffee percolator drips staining time
pages so blank
I have to fill it with something

all those witnesses who could not stop it
I write down what they say
and sometimes what's unsaid

Sisters

I measure the distance
between where I stand
and where she lies.
I remember gravity.
The words mouthed aloud:
ashes, dust.
Every tear I taste on my tongue
salts grief.
I think of warm lips
on a cold cheek.
Flesh into bone.
I doubt and finger
her bullet-holes —
obscene mouths
that speak for her.

Dumb

baby brother brings me booty
booty I do not want
blood out of squirrels' mouths
blooms from a badger's back
broke spine splinter bones
blown wide apart
belly open of a fine snout fox
bleached fur stiff fuzz
better not show baby brother
briny pinpoint pupils' glaze

brings me his killing jar
bees, spiders, hornets and wasps
brave his fingertips' acetone smell
dumb husks in a glass shell

The Mistress speaks

i

Nothing out of the ordinary happened
when we met.
Not thunder or the plague.
Neither locusts nor hail.

He liked
me.
I liked
him.

My husband,
his wife:
the possessives no longer applied.
So we kept at it until he died.

ii

My lover was calm without her name around
and gentle with me.
This was our house. I'd stand at the sink,
wait for him to come whistling.

He never said what one says.
He'd get as quiet as my rifle cabinet.
All locked up.
I had the key.

iii

They're not that hard to use.
Point and shoot.
Unbolt the stock, stick in the bucks, aim and fire.

As many as seven times....
That's what I'd read.
You think you know a man.
I guess I didn't.

What cruel surprise.
Like bats flying in the night,
some things can barely be heard or seen:
the barely inaudible flapping of wings.

There were no signs
anywhere. Everywhere
there were signs.
If only I'd seen.

Who pays attention to everything?
People say bad things about me
and the money that's coming. I pay attention.
I overhear things.

I was not curious enough.
Maybe I should've asked.
To me, he was a man coming down a gravel path,
knife-sharp and kind.

Rinsing fillets at the sink,
so pink in my hands.
The lemon juice had the tang
of regret. I ignored it,
even as it stung
the cut on my finger.

The rice was plump and blameless.
Turmeric stains my hands yellow.
drips down white walls in a slick gout.

vi

He liked to stun butterflies
with formaldehyde.
Any bigger and I'd
kill them, too.

vii

This is the sum.
I know all about
what adds up.
All day I file and file,

sign and sign.
The oven timer said
it's almost time.
These are the rules.

The fluttering of my viscera
betrays me,
like he did
when he did what he did.

I may be the fulcrum.
I am implicated in this.
He copied my keys.
Stole my rifle from me.

It will always add up.
I know the law.
The oven dings.
It's time.

A Priest thinks on his future

If I handle this right
this might make my name:
a double murder–suicide
does not happen everyday
– not among my parishioners, anyway.

Should I say,
'This is a testing time
for me as a priest…'?

Or 'The deceased
were wonderful people'?
I should say more about me.

Hundreds in the chapel,
tears glittering in the aisles,
salt in a hundred palms,
grief shining in their eyes.
Stained glass windows all alight.

Coughs and shuffles echo
up the nave,
those cold heights.

Black dust gathers in the corners.
Many candles burning,
melting white.

Hundreds looking at me:
reporters, relatives, parishioners.
And me, a mere priest.

My voice will soar like that holy bird.
How they'll swallow my every word.

The Detective Inspector I

it was difficult to find you in the dark
there were notes
clues
but our lights could not find you
not right away
and we arrived too late for rescue
we know
the gravel underfoot
a bed of breadcrumbs
we stumble around

the stars whir too loudly
the stiff smoke of fireworks
something liquid collects under a cheek
drips and falls
a moth butts against a bulb
the pines shake their needles to the floor
the windows outstare the moon

think of the worst
I think to myself
twist the handle
open the door

The Detective Inspector II

— eyes make
in
cre
mental
adjustments
in the dark

trees?
or walls?
hard to judge

the pointed pines stand in a row
watch & whisper
hard to know
where threat or danger
lies

— death can walk up to you
with your father's face
or your husband's voice

would've felt the trigger
against his finger
and that was the last of it

— I was the investigating officer.
We knew about his threats.
We did what we could.
We did not know the situation.
We did not want to lose our men.
It was hard to find in the dark.

The Four Policemen

Policeman I

There was a lot we didn't know.
Our uniforms still had the itch of starch,
rubbing our necks raw.
We weren't to know.

Everything too shiny.
We didn't want to go.
The moon would have picked us out.
We weren't to know

he was there,
killing them as we waited to go.
The cold gripped the air in our throats.
It looked like snow

clouds waiting, as we were.
Shotgun shots—one, two, three, four.
We stayed right there.
Five, six, maybe more.

We were still so new.
It's no excuse.
Nobody knew what to do.
It was no use.

Policeman II

She kept calling us, calling for help.
Not shrill, no,
but reedy as a note blown over water.

We gave her what protection we could.
We gave her our words.
We can only do so much.

Her dress, for instance, did not shield her
from the buckshot aimed at her front and back.
We do what we can.

Life is life. Yes. Nothing can be changed.
Nothing more can be done or said.
She rang and rang.

We do what we can.

Policeman III

When I went past the gates,
I didn't really know
what I was looking at.
I'd never seen a dead one before.

He was a young boy.
Same as my brother.
Same age.
He had a hole

here
and here.
And his hands, too,
red and holey

from trying to stop
gravity happening.
On the gravel
fallen down

head aside
to cough or speak,
all his red
between rough stones,

drying brown.
Lashes open to the sky,
eyes full of dew or rain
he couldn't blink away.

Policeman IV

the house was difficult
to find in the dark
everything conspired
against us and you.

the absence of light
turned gleams into eyes
flashes were bullets
aimed at heads or hearts

so you died
in blanket darkness
warm as the wool
you no longer need

your son coated
with dried blood
flakes falling
as we lift his body

five wounds
blood and bone
red and white
his chest a cavity

and you no longer cold
arms by your sides
curled inside
the smallest space

your back to us
face to the wall
white spine poking
through the holes

found by your killer
with the door open
we touch your blood
we tread on it

upstairs downstairs
evidence everywhere
outlines of the people
you used to be

we gather clues and traces
as if we loved you
storing you
in plastic bags

The Police Surgeon's tale

i

I've come to know people
through their bodies, their wounds
the way the blood moves as I drain it out

the body's decay can say so much
the flesh is a page I read and read

there is order and procedure
to corral the chaos
of homicide

checklists and questions to ask
sign my name
on flawless paper

my lab coat is always white and pure
I have learned not to stain it
with the body's fluids

every little thing shows up
in the right light
blood fluoresces blue
even when you think it's been wiped
clean away

ii

an easy case of a killer
whose blood was up
planned his killing to the last drop
shotgun cartridges petrol can
rope vodka cable ties
all in hand
plan a plan b
suicide note
explaining himself to himself
no doubt about it

no rescue for her
or the son
not when it was time

iii

I rue September
– the chaos of the season.
Something's always changing.

Suicide and homicide
– evil twins of my business.

How to separate the two
squabbling siblings.
How to tell them apart.

iv

I am taken
to the outer cordon.
A stretch of tape
flickers in the wind.
Beyond is hallowed ground
– I step in.
Survey the scene.
My eye fixes bodies in their spaces.

The boy.

Urgent strobe lights
open and shut their eyes:
keep away keep away

The mother
upstairs
hidden in a cupboard
a jar of glacé cherries
broken back
half in, half out
the door
blood on the floor

Unlike the father
who dispatched himself more efficiently
a neat fountain spray of remorse
above his head
stained halo

Move the bodies
to the mortuary
perform the autopsy
where I can see for myself
how everything's undone

v

Everything must be weighed.
Everything accounted for.
Every pinprick, every scratch.
My eye is a microscope,
more meticulous than God.

Family portrait

My hair has a showroom shine. My husband
prefers it long. Benign as a leash. I smile and
smile. Keeping mum. Keeping clean.

His arm: heavy on my back. My daughter
kneels. My son beside me.

In the pot plant, a beetle dies. Its legs kick
slowly. There is a dark stain on the carpet.
The flashbulb burns my eyes.

The last time I felt pretty was a long time ago.

The family friend

Here in case of emergency
like a bandage or a splint
a stitch for the cut lip
a steak for the black eye
or a white lie at the hospital
to blame the door
the stairs
or clumsiness

I am the call to the domestic violence unit

I am the small panic button
that's pressed and pressed again

A year of death threats

the hours
tea-stained

we wait
saucers cracking against cups

Happy Sunday: Jane

i

most mornings
before he wakes
I'm a cupful of birdsong

ii

I read today's fortune
in a glass of water
in beads that cling
like seeds of mercury
his distorted face
watches me

A small domestic scene

'Blood comes out in cold water,'
he said to me,
almost tenderly,
from the doorway,
as I held the icepack to my cheek,
looked at my blouse in the mirror,
fingered the stains.

Warning

at the private hospital bed
she said *divorce*
her face staring at the wall

a nurse overheard
embarrassed or bored
I couldn't tell

she picked the right time
she had her witness
fine, I said

besides
I have someone else
my very own mistress

and though she tried to hide it
I could see
her eyes smoothing out
her body unknotting with relief

you can even keep the house
I said with a smile

then I leaned in to kiss her
to graze her ear and whisper
before she could even flinch

but you can't keep my children from me
they're mine
and I decide

I decide.

The Journalist speaks III

I'm at the crime scene
watching dusk's cloud calligraphy

my pen makes thoughts real
the ink sets it down so I can forget it
and so reshape it
into something that makes sense

erase the smell of blood and cordite
the look of bone as it breaks through skin
the final mask the face will wear

the feel of the page
                        smooth and blameless
takes everything I can give it
gives everyone a new identity
                                even me
away from the taste of stale coffee
spiked with whiskey

all complexity flattened to a headline
'Three shot dead in village'

Black cameras crowd in,
flashbulbs white as maggots.
She gives them a flat, dry stare,
the surviving daughter who releases her statement.

Signatures

I was sure
I was dying a slow death
who knows if this would hasten it
my decision
to take the paper
and sign, sign, sign
in triplicate to make it real
to make him feel it where it hurts
change the locks and tell it true
all those bruises
his ruse – I wasn't clumsy
just tongue-tied
well, I'm undoing the knot
that held my breath for fifteen years
my daughter might come back
my son might smile again
and all I have to do
is seal this envelope
slip it in the slot
let drop
from my suddenly nerveless hand

Tom alone

in my room
by the window
I can feel the sun's heat
on the other side of the glass

my warmth leaching from me
my temperature dropping slowly

my big sister   gone
and I alone must face our father

the way he doesn't see me
just my mother

how he'd fight her
over stains
that aren't there

her survival tactic   to go limp
her mind moving on
an embarrassed guest closing the door

his strange vulpine smile

I know one day there'll come a time
when he'll finally see me

and I don't know
if I'll be ready

Hannah's statement

i

I would like to clarify
the darkness that surrounds me
and those whom I loved,
the fine soot that clung –
I cannot shake it off.

I remember each bruise
their particular truth
their radius of pain

somehow I escaped
the blasted landscape of our lives
where I learnt to stay low to the ground
be numb
survive

ii

once   after my brother ran
he placed my hand on his heart
fat sparrow in a ribcage
skin glowing like a hotplate

I asked him
how does it feel

he said to breathe is to burn

I should've asked
how he kept on running
heart and lungs near-bursting
hair a cloud full of sweat

what was the engine that drove him
on and on again
not away
from father   mother   our strange half-life
but towards a hallucination

like water shimmering when you're thirsty
to never fill your mouth

Jane's to-do list

1. spring clean

I have been told to eliminate dust.
Keep a clean house. Bite down my tongue. Air, blood,
chemicals in my lungs. Bleached perfection.
Shrill ammonia. Add soap and water.
Everything polished to a worry bead.

Every flat surface glares into my eyes.
Feel dumb; stunned; half-blind. Go around by touch,
inward as a pulse, the walls plumb and true.
Who am I in these rooms? – Bed, bath and pantry,
living, dining and conservatory,
kitchen, sewing, basement, reception, den.

Prefer the interstitial life: wait out
in corridors, hallways, passages, stairs.
Who else would notice the black bread burning
in the toaster? An indelible smell

seeps into the walls. There's no end. And all
my careful cakes and pastries, my averted
gazes, my shadow industry won't stop
him from hitting me, even killing me,

and I know he'll do it eventually.

2. ask about Hannah's room

My daughter's doll's dress's hem is dusty:
the shelf furred with neglect. With a head
bigger than its body, hollow and blank.

A threaded needle dangling, divining
the baby in me. Girl goes 'round, boy up–
down, or side to side. One girl. Then one boy.

Did a line of silver tell my future?
This I know. I never wanted to be
what I've become: a doll inside a doll

inside a doll. Dust motes settle on plastic hair.
I know that same blue-eyed stare. The eyes show
the brushstrokes. I know how moths

can eat at one's abbreviated clothes.
Unbending arms that stay right where they are.
Picked up and put down. Anybody's whim.

Lie me down, I close my eyes. Stand me up,
my lids flick open. Take everything in.
I keep my secret tattooed under skin.

3. book beauty treatment

Too open-faced. Plain as a plate, a napkin.
Somebody else. A pinprick self.
A sliver that melts. Thinned to a splinter.
In the dark.
A needle spinner.

Scolded for crookedness,
I tried to cut it straight.
But my hair would disobey.

drag my finger against my skin along and up my
cheek   reverse   time's   inexorable   wreck
wrinkles go back slack muscles tighten frown
lines disappear from my eyes the crow unsteps
its tracks mistakes are unmade my young self
returned to me again

more lines than freckles
a mouth that smiles less

uncreased unstained
no bruises no pain
all blood inside me

4. replace broken mirror

I was raised on polite silences
my daily bread
my long hair shed and combed and bound again
my gaze lowered
my hands quiet
the pulse at my wrists a lie
this seemed the pattern of my life
learn to lie down
let myself be poured into
this strange shape
called wife

5. find locksmith

black blades of grass
sharpen underfoot
undulled by falling dew

nightly the stars
as the sound of crickets' legs
rub in the dark
sing their song of light years
to reach me

6. get advice

his eyes on my skin
two slugs silvering

the breast he touched and loved so much
I cut it out

failed Amazon

you can't break
what is already broken

7. write down everything

once upon a time
a lady lay unconscious on the floor

when she came to, she knew
her knight had come and knocked her down

with a swole eye, she lied
to anyone who asked

8. re-stock fridge

raspberry ripple ice-cream
blood on skin

dried grape juice
an older bruise

blueberry stain
shoulder sprain

the door's sharp edge
fed to my face

you deserve it
he said

9. write out next week's to-do list

I must not bruise
I must not bleed
I must not speak
I must not scream

Divorce

I feel myself give the world
my dead eyes
my slow wife
oh, she fooled me, all right
see the panicked glitter in her eyes
she nods and smiles

doesn't she remember our vows?
only one word can part us
not a lawyer but the law of blood
now something
is about to happen

Tony

first

There is no explanation for me.
The whisper in the dark.

The sky hangs upside down in a pitcher of water.
Trees miniature and condensed
       their dizzying fronds
       their green
       the clouds not at all astonished
       the copper beech

second

In golf, there is the swing.
Three hundred and fifty-three
     dimples in a golf ball.
The air in every one sends it flying.
I am the fulcrum
     the pendulum
     the force for the perfect arc.
Believe it.
I like to really hit it
         clear out
         become the swing
         that propels   to the far, far green.

third

Real things seem untouchable to me
                                    my life
                                    my family
Sometimes I tell the truth
but really crave the lie.

Believe it.

Truth is a shadow
wavering on a wall,
dust that skims
across your eyeballs.

Belief can evaporate
            like water
            just apply pressure
            heat
            time

fourth

The dark seam
The hanging breath
That red mist coming over me
        when she makes me angry
        just by being there
Her look of kick me
        bruise me
        hit me

The state of her

A fly crawls along the wall
        watching me
        through the glass

A dark vitality
        inside me
        crawls along
        my inner walls
        and I pass for someone ordinary
        someone who looks   like me

fifth

I usher out the flies
                which return
                        keep returning
                disappear into wallpaper—
their shiny and several
                thirty-eight eyes
                        watch me as the cold
                comes through the window—
they beat themselves
                against the glass
                        and the wood
                warps itself
from too much—
                something unknown
                        (perhaps)
                attracted by
my breath

the stain of my hand
                on her jaw
                        bruising
                darkening
disappearing
                down
                        several
                days

a fly flying off
                the moving charcoal
                        smudge of itself
                the dull gold
glamour of love
                I cannot
                      fathom it

she lets them go
                she lets them go
                      on their own
                not knowing
how much it costs me

sixth

this is the dark
    I know
         chasing me
         down the road
the double-tongued bark
      the noisome shout

         I don't know
         how it took me
      but it did
one minute
I was there
      the next
         I'm downhill
         falling over
      into dark water
mud sucking at my feet
dragging me down

      the subdermal itch
         I'll never
         stop scratching
      always watching
never stopping
the dark
      always coming
         a veil over me
         dimly glimpsed
      the truth of myself
a whisper of words
in an unknowable tongue

      the spike of attention
         the boiling blood

      something chases me down
         always chasing me down

seventh

the sticky pitch

rolling black tears
I am at the edge of the road

tar squeezed out from lungs
bread gone bad with mould

rank
bin juice

there
a drift of milk
  white seed pods
  float past

  a flock of wishes
  a child might have cast
                    out

brown-eyed child
misshapen inside
hands steeped red
lining torn
club-footed soul
                    and hare-lipped too
some unwanted thing
like a knot in the thread

one pull
and the sky punches through

something and nothing
like a river of monoxide
a whisper of a threat
an intimation of death

something and nothing inside me
a hunger gnawing
not knowing what to do
                    next

eighth

at night I dream of red
mist crawls from the river to claim me
at night red *becomes* me
all the time I am red
all the time red claims me
red I am red I am red
all over drenched in red
sleeping in red screams the red
throat white eyes the sound my fist
makes when it hits her cheek
wakes me right up to feel finally alive

the smell of her fear-stained sweat
the taste of it is blood on my tongue
the dull tang of rust and iron
something in my heart does not work
its clock-gears failed
console myself with the bare mechanics
breathe in
breathe out
don't lose the trick of it
not until you're ready for it

I'm only electric when she's close to death

ninth

I am not much for speeches.
I tend to just watch.
The tongue is a trap.
You can say too much.

When I hunt, I am quiet.
I like to hide and not be seen.
Sometimes the prey comes to you.
This is what I've seen.
This is what I know.
Prepare.
As much as you can.

When I hunt, I am more myself
than ever.
No longer an unsuitable man.
I am my own best version then.
No longer an ordinary sort.
Ordinary sweat of an ordinary man.

Better to be a brute
than be far less.
I realise myself

when I hunt.

tenth

little things can set me off
I hardly know myself when I go off

thin red mist
hot and fine
before my eyes

my accountant's hands become these fists
      that rightly fit
      the hollow of her cheek
      her belly
      her ribs
and I know myself to be
      finally true
      to me.

eleventh

I smell me and the harsh acid survives in sweat to smell the sour
accretions of the day and a life that apes to be normal bleach
might fix things that boiled pork fat smell almost rancid and off
two day old socks and stale whiff of sadness the only thing to
stop this rage is blood a red exclamation mark across a page
petrol rope plastic ties be prepared I say be prepared petrol for a
pyre turn it all to ash rope to tie them back ties that bind so flesh
turns white she won't get away she won't fucking well get away
I'll be damned and anyone else who gets in the way
of this

twelfth

I see the end of it
my hands at my side
one holds death's hand
white and shaped like a shotgun
long and kindly
brings rest to the restless
minds like mine
brings peace to others
pain giving way
to the long sleep
cradled and taken away
– the final nothing

Notes to self

1. Go to hardware store:
   - rope, ties, garden hose
   - pliers, blowtorch, metal wire
   - shovel, tarpaulin, hammer, nails
   - nail gun

2. Check supplies:
   - five boxes, red cartridges
   - 12-gauge shotgun (need to clean?)
   - spare rifle?

3. Go to locksmith
   - duplicate key to N's gun cabinet

4. Write last notes
   - one to lawyer
   - one to leave behind

5. Withdraw money.

6. Check car.

7. Dinner with N (mention my divorce, sign papers)

8. Sunday: Golf. Break in new nine-iron.

9. Act normal.

Tom

Here is my armour, the lineaments of my uniform. My inhuman hormones take hold of me again, so gangly and indestructible. Turning into the man by turning against the man I don't want to be. I know I'm doomed now. Every shoelace I tie is undone, frays sadly imperfect and black. Every night a full moon, white and staring in, an irisless eyeball – glaucoma or ghosts.... The pines whisper out there, in a huddle. Their needles point at me. I am chosen. And all I have to do is run.

The smell of rain before the rain, rising swampy across oily asphalt.... My feet hit and hit and hit their mark every time. My breath, my lungs, meet each other in synchrony, farther and farther 'til there is nothing here I know but the horizon, and the sun burns the bones of my back, my shoulders.

Too exposed. Bird bones, uncovered, shrugging off, month by month, feathers and skin, the sky looking in at the body's slim architecture.

My left arm up; my right arm by my side.... The sky's in my eyes and sees itself upside down, a glossy cosmos.

Mother calls and calls and my name fills my ears like water.

I could lose myself, drop down a well of notes and song. Echo me in my chamber – walled in.

The stars are far from my life. *The shouts and angry eyes, their knife points of light fill my head, crowd out the bad bad bad, leave no room for thinking, of doing him in, of killing him when he's not looking, my own hands must do something else besides what it wants to do.*

the mud smudge of camouflage
the old dead hides
he taught me invisibility
to get closer to the kill.

I learned
check it twice
do it once
get it right then be gone
and get away
clean

Witness

We're laughing – a rare thing.
After dinner and we're at the sink.
We hear a car on the gravel drive. Our laughter dries.

In the living room, we turn off the lights,
see the car, catch each other's eye. It's him.

Minutes pass. A shadow moves.
Shotgun silhouette.
I can't stop shivering.
Tom shoves me towards the phone,
runs outside and locks me in.
He's gone. My son
and his father with a shotgun. I hear
my son
yell at his father,
my husband yell at his son.

Shouting. Shouting.
My hands are shaking. My fingers don't work.

He cracks the rifle in half,
slides one shell down each barrel. Snaps it whole again.
Raises the sight to his eye.

My son runs. His father tracks him with his gun.

Something loud echoes in the trees.
Someone is screaming. I think it's me.
I'm running in the house,

upstairs, downstairs.
Looking for somewhere to hide
away.

Tony and Tom

he knows that silhouette
heart starts its slow beat
feet carry him to the door
into breath–fogged air

a son tells his father
to leave
go on home
that's not here anymore

legs locked so's not to crumple
eyes widen and flicker
rising smell of ethanol

a shotgun moves into the light

chest bursting
he pulls on his father's arm
a slim block of flesh
the stars look on
this has nothing to do with them

his father gives a warning
it fades to nothing

Tom braces himself
to run
a slow charge
his yelling breath
bells from his lips
his face

glows
lights the new stubble below
the hectic crescents of his cheeks
long lashes at his brow
the white around
the staring iris of his eye
his open right hand dries
sweat in the night air

father   son
    an arm's length apart

finger and trigger do their work
the slugs race up the barrel

Tom catches his breath
staggers
Dad
you missed
he runs

sound on sound

hot bouquets
brief night flowers

something wet
and red

See Jane run

Tom runs outside the house. Tom is Jane's son. Tom is Dick's son. See Tom run. Run, Tom, run.

Tom sees Dick. Dick sees Tom. Tom yells at Dick. 'Stop, Dad, stop.' See Dick stop. Watch Dick run. Dick has a gun. See Tom run. Run, Tom, run.

Watch Dick chase Tom. See Dick run. See Tom run. Watch Dick shoot his gun. Tom yells at Dick. 'Stop, Dad, stop.' Hear Tom cry. Tom tries to run. Run, Tom, run. Watch Dick shoot his gun. Watch Dick shoot his son.

Watch Tom die. Hear Tom die. Hear Jane cry. See Jane run and hide.

See Jane run. Watch Dick run. Watch Dick chase Jane. Watch Dick chase Jane through their house. Dick has a gun. Run, Jane, run. Run, Dick, run.

Dick is mad. Dick yells at Jane. 'Stop, Jane, stop.' Jane sees the gun. Jane sees Dick and runs. Run, Jane, run. Jane runs and hides. Watch Jane hide. Watch Jane hide from Dick. Run, Jane, run.

See Dick look for Jane. See Jane hide. Run, Dick, run. Hide, Jane, hide.

Holes

I pressed the button. No-one came. The police could not find me in the dark. They were also afraid of death... it might come for them instead. They waited behind a screen of trees, for the moon to uncover itself, silver the edges of their sirens, their dark cars. The pale pebbles in the driveway, left to imagine the river that used to wet them – they must tire of always staring up, sightless and at the mercy of everything. The police step on them. They creep only so close, but no closer. My son is dead on the ground. Someone close his eyes. But I am ignored in this as I have been with so many other things. His blood is cold now, blackening, drying up, stiffening the fabric of his jacket, soaking into the soil. There are holes in him I know nothing about, nothing to do with the boy I delivered to the world, my gift, small and pure. The dark is blue and cold. The trees conceal susurrations in their high skirts, branches uplifted like arms, wailing whispers... black cars, old scars, my son's open mouth, empty shotgun shells whistling smoke white dancing up and out

The Journalist's tale

A man pulls up in his car.
In the trunk, he has stashed ropes, plastic ties, petrol and other assorted implements.
On the seat next to him are bottles of alcohol, wads of cash, a shotgun and boxes of shotgun shells.
He sits in his car while a neighbour from the house next door watches him.
The man talks to himself, sometimes hitting the steering wheel for emphasis, sometimes raking fingers through his hair, drinks from the bottle with a deep swig.
He keeps his eyes on the lights of a gated house.

Inside the house, a mother and son watch the car from a window.
There is a moon.
There are pine trees.
There is a man outside their house, who used to be the man of the house.
The light from the moon and some street lamps show the man getting out of the car.

He never takes his eyes off the house.

A neighbour's lights go off, closes his curtains.

The man watches the house as he
ns against the car.
ther and son watch the man.

The pine trees shift uneasily.
A cloud blows itself across the moon's face.
A low-voiced dog starts barking.
The mother goes to the phone and calls the police.

The man pushes from the car, opens one of the car doors and gets his shotgun out.
The son goes to the door of the house.
The man opens up the shotgun, loads two shells into the barrels, locks it in place.
He empties boxes and stuffs handfuls of shells in his pockets.
He slams the door shut.

The man starts to walk toward the house.

The son is out the door, down the steps and running towards the man, who has just gone past the gates and stepped on the gravel path.
The mother talks to the phone operator at the police station, just as her son runs outside to meet the man, his father, her husband.

The mother sees her son run.
The son, heart beating fast from the run, from fear, from sudden flight, taunts the man into giving chase, away from the house and his mother inside.
The man aims.

Fires twice.

The mother cries.
The operator can hear the shots.

The son staggers, falls to his knees, gets up to run.
The operator asks for the mother's address, as she locks the door of her house.

The man loads more shells.
Aims.
Fires.
Fires.

The woman runs through the house.
Upstairs, downstairs.

Her son bleeds.

More words.

The man loads more shotgun shells.
Aims.
Fires.

The mother runs for the basement.

The son lies on the gravel path.
Blood bubbles in his mouth, slips quietly from the wounds in his sides.

The man fishes for more shells.
Once more, he turns toward the house.

The mother cannot lock the door

to the basement – there is no lock.
The man tries to break down the front door.
The mother sees an empty cupboard and gets inside.
The man goes to the side, sees a window and shoots it.
The glass falls apart.

The mother closes the cupboard door – there is no lock.
The man runs through the house, calling her name, calling her whore, bitch, slut, cunt, saying he'll kill her, he'll kill her.
The operator tells her to stay where she is – keep hidden.

For the longest time, silence.

In a matter of seconds, silence fills the space of a month.

It is the silence of communion.
Between hunter and hunted.

Then the laboured breath that betrays the silence.

The eyes that flicker in the dark, that judge and make adjustments.

The hand that waits and the heart that beats.

My lover as a ghost
or the Mistress speaks again

it is the smell that rises
from upturned earth
returned
compressed by your body's weight

the taste of your body's salt
wells from secret places
a different glitter to sea salt,
Algerian salt, the Red Sea

my throat's lining burned
raw skin tags
nerves leaping
for the voiceless scream

my eyes' willing self-deception
creates a body from shadow
how my eyes love you so
it doubles you from nothing

the brush of your heels against carpet
our fricative limbs rolling over
the question in the room
the raised inflection I cannot answer

The surviving Daughter

i

I can get used to swallowing the dead.
Take them on my tongue.
Their weight   loosening
the sigh in my lungs.

There is a sun behind those clouds,
Mother said. Sadness dispersing,
like a drop of dark matter
falling in clear water.

Father was never happy
even with perfection.
No-one knew where he was going
or where he went.
Always gone.
Always there
with his stares.
The bruises he gave
in the curve of her eyes.
Colours receding after awhile
like tide retreating from the shore,
mist or fog rising from the woods.

I never wanted to be there,
that place they called home.
The low drone of days,
the inevitable.
The slug inches along,
waiting for the wet days.

Brightest and best.

So I left
as soon as I could
the black cloud
of home.

Lines across paper.
The lecturer's drone.
My classmate's snore.
The length of my hair
                    marking time.
A rope to hang.
A discarded web
                    and the spider long gone.
At night, the oak
drops black dust over all things.
Powdered shadows.   Sooty mould.
The opposite of chalk.
Opposite of salt on skin.
Acorns like strewn knuckles:
knurled hats
and polished coats.

I am transfixed in halls
by escape maps, safe routes.
'You are here.'
Red trace around a house.
Marked-out walls   and the promise of rescue.

ii

Colour drains from photographs.
The family portrait
        a scam
        a sham
        a ramshackle arrangement
people thrown together
by accident
an imitation of happiness
stilted rictus grins
the shining hair
a hand on a shoulder bruising
the mark on a piece of fruit

the raised arm
the fended blow
the spittle drops
the insults
how he called her   me   her
        whore
        whore
        fucking whore
one's slim wrist can only defend so much

Now their death is a stone
weight upon weight on my breastbone
squeezing my breath
shut, open, shut.

Acknowledgements

Thanks to the editors of *Brilliant Coroners* (Montreal: Phoenicia Publishing, 2007), *Deconstructions, A Face to Meet the Faces* (University of Akron Press, 2012), FOURSQUARE, *Galatea Resurrects*, *Going Down Swinging*, *Loose Muse* (Flipped Eye, 2013), *Mimesis*, *OCHO*, *Roundyhouse*, *The Seoul International Writers' Festival* (Literature Translation Institute of Korea, 2012), *Veils, Halos and Shackles* (eds. Charles Fishman and Smita Sahay) and *Words on the Web*.

Deepest gratitude to MacDowell Colony, Hawthornden Castle, the Australia Council for the Arts, Literature Wales, the Tyrone Guthrie Centre and Fundación Valparaíso for the gift of time to write this book.

Thank you, Nick Carbó, Teju Cole, Simon Hicks, Adam Hyland, Philippa Moore, Sally Spedding and Amy Wack.

Australian Government

This project has been assisted by the Australian Government through the Australia Council, its arts funding and advisory body.

Llenyddiaeth
Cymru
Literature
Wales

The author wishes to acknowledge the award of a Writer's Bursary from Literature Wales for the purpose of completing this collection.

Author Note

Ivy Alvarez is the author of *Mortal* (Washington, DC: Red Morning Press, 2006), her first poetry collection. Her poems appear in anthologies, journals and new media in many countries, including *Poetry Wales, New Welsh Review, Roundyhouse, Scintilla* and *Red Poets*, as well as *Best Australian Poems* (2009), *A Face to Meet the Faces* (University of Akron Press, 2012), *The Guardian* (online, 2012), *Prairie Schooner* (US, 2012) and *Junctures* (NZ, 2010), with individual poems translated into Russian, Spanish, Japanese and Korean. A MacDowell and Hawthornden Fellow thrice-shortlisted for Best Poem by *fourW* (Australia), both Literature Wales and the Australia Council for the Arts awarded grants towards the writing of *Disturbance*.

SEREN

Well chosen words

Seren is an independent publisher with a wide-ranging list which includes poetry, fiction, biography, art, translation, criticism and history. Many of our books and authors have been shortlisted for – or won – major literary prizes, among them the Costa Award, the Man Booker, Forward Prize, and TS Eliot Prize.

At the heart of our list is a good story told well or an idea or history presented interestingly or provocatively. We're international in authorship and readership though our roots are here in Wales (Seren means Star in Welsh), where we prove that writers from a small country with an intricate culture have a worldwide relevance.

Our aim is to publish work of the highest literary and artistic merit that also succeeds commercially in a competitive, fast changing environment. You can help us achieve this goal by reading more of our books – available from all good bookshops and increasingly as e-books. You can also buy them at 20% discount from our website, and get monthly updates about forthcoming titles, readings, launches and other news about Seren and the authors we publish.

www.serenbooks.com

a. 4. 14